# Meet Your Teeth

## A Fun, Creative Dental Care Unit
## for Kids in Grades 1–4

**Written by Linda Schwartz • Illustrated by Kelly Kennedy**

# The Learning Works

*Cover Design & Illustration:*
Kelly Kennedy

*Edited by:*
Barbara Christie-Dever and Kimberley A. Clark

*Text Design and Editorial Production:*
Clark Editorial & Design

## Acknowledgments

Special thanks to
Dr. Dennis Mann, D.D.S.,
Dr. Kenneth L. Gaynes, D.D.S., and
Dr. Robert J. Kuhn, D.D.S., M.S.D. and his staff.
Thanks also to Chris and David Persson.

Creative Teaching Press, Inc.
Huntington Beach, CA 92649

ISBN: 0-88160-274-4
Library of Congress: 95-080496

# Contents

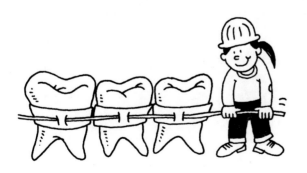

Meet Your Teeth
© The Learning Works, Inc.

# Introduction

### To Teachers

*Meet Your Teeth* is a fun, creative way for kids to learn about their teeth and dental health. This thematic unit is geared for kids in grades 1–4 and incorporates all areas of the curriculum—reading, research, writing, poetry, spelling, science, and art as well as creative thinking skills. The book contains more than fifty pages of activities and information on topics such as brushing and flossing, identifying the parts of a tooth, eating healthy, and learning about routine dental procedures.

*Meet Your Teeth* is packed with puzzles, word games, codes, word searches, and more for your students and time-saving pages for you such as dental clip art, awards, and certificates.

Although the book can be used all year long, it is especially appropriate during National Children's Dental Health Month and National Dental Hygiene Week.

### To Parents

*Meet Your Teeth* is the ideal way to help your child learn good dental hygiene at home. It's easy to use, fun for kids, and filled with helpful information. When it's time for your child to visit the dentist, go through the book together. The information and activities explain what happens during a routine dental exam, including x-rays, cleaning, flossing, and filling of teeth. There are also activities to teach your child about the proper foods to eat for healthy teeth, puzzles to solve, and art and puppet projects to reinforce dental facts your child has learned.

When working together with your child, just do a few pages at a sitting. The length of time you work together will vary depending on the age, maturity level, and attention span of your child.

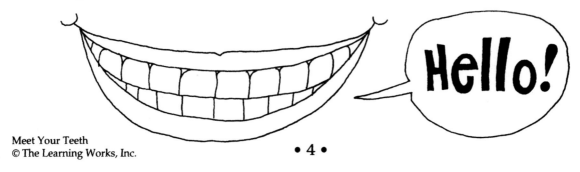

# Why Are Teeth Important?

Teeth are made of special kinds of bone cells. They grow in your upper and lower jawbones. Teeth have several important uses.

Teeth are used to bite and chew food. As you chew your food, it is mixed with saliva, making it wet and easier for you to swallow. If you didn't have any teeth, you could only eat soft foods. Think of all the fun you'd miss if you couldn't eat steaks, corn-on-the-cob, carrots, and other yummy foods!

Your teeth also help you talk. Your tongue, lips, and teeth work together to form many sounds that make up words. For example, notice how your tongue presses against the back of your top teeth when you say the word "the."

Teeth help to support the muscles around your mouth. They make an important difference in the way you look.

YOUR TEETH

Meet Your Teeth
© The Learning Works, Inc.

# Parts of a Tooth

When you look at a tooth, the only part you can see is the top part called the **crown**. But each tooth has **roots** that are hidden from view by your gums. These roots go deep into your jawbone and hold your teeth in place. Gums cover your jawbones like skin.

Your teeth are covered with **enamel** (ee-NAM-ul). The enamel protects your teeth and makes them look shiny and white. The enamel is the hardest part of your entire body.

Under the enamel is a very hard layer of **dentin** (DEN-tin). Inside the dentin layer is a spongy material called **pulp**, which contains **nerves** and **blood vessels**. Nerves are like wires that carry messages and feelings to and from your brain. Blood vessels are the tubes that carry blood to all parts of your body.

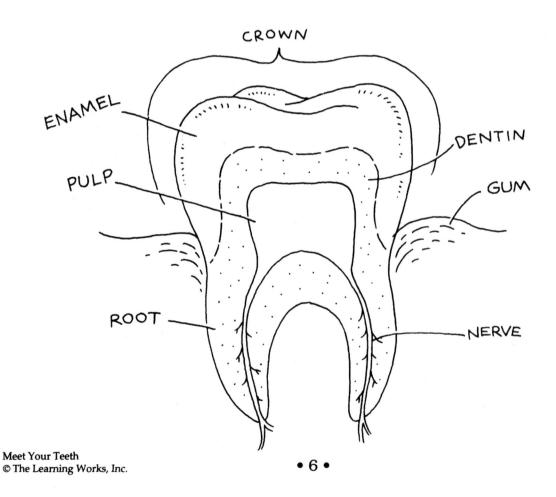

# Baby and Permanent Teeth

Did you know that there are two sets of teeth that develop in your mouth? The first set is the **primary teeth**, often called "baby teeth" or "milk teeth." These teeth begin **erupting** (ee-RUPT-ing), or coming out of the gums, when babies are about five or six months old. These primary teeth are important because they hold space in the jaw for the teeth that will later replace them. There are twenty teeth in this primary set.

**Permanent teeth** first start to appear at about six years of age. Between the ages of six and twelve, baby teeth are pushed out and are replaced by the permanent teeth growing beneath them. When they have all grown in, there are usually 32 teeth in this set.

If you have lost any of your primary teeth, you may have noticed that they have no roots. Well, they *did* have roots, but when your permanent teeth began to grow into place, the roots of the primary teeth dissolved!

• 7 •

# Kinds of Teeth

There are four kinds of teeth. Each has a different shape, and each is used for a different purpose.

## INCISORS

**Incisors** are teeth used for cutting food. Permanent incisors replace primary incisors between ages six and nine.

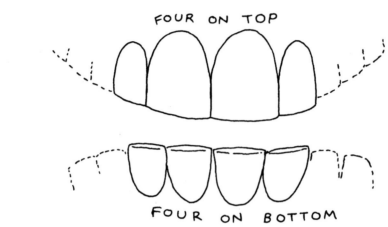

FOUR ON TOP

FOUR ON BOTTOM

## CUSPIDS OR CANINES

**Cuspids,** or **canines,** are pointed teeth used for ripping and tearing food into smaller pieces. Permanent cuspids replace primary cuspids between the ages of seven and nine.

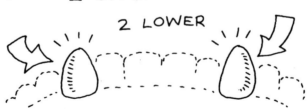

2 UPPER

2 LOWER

# Kinds of Teeth
## (continued)

### BICUSPIDS

**Bicuspids** have two sharp points that help crunch and shred food into smaller pieces. They erupt when you are ten to twelve years old.

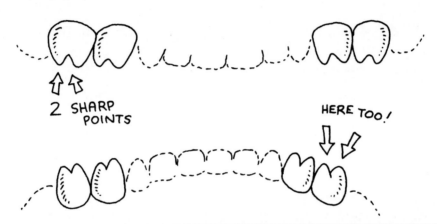

2 SHARP POINTS

HERE TOO!

### MOLARS

**Molars** are your back teeth. They have large, grooved surfaces that are used to mash and grind food. Permanent molars erupt around the time you are six, twelve, and eighteen years old. Your last molars, called **wisdom teeth**, sometimes don't erupt at all.

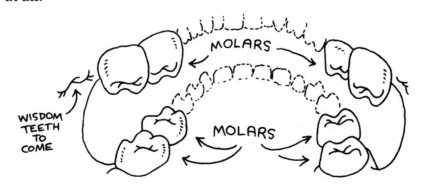

MOLARS

WISDOM TEETH TO COME

MOLARS

• 9 •

# What Causes Tooth Decay?

**Decay** means to break down or rot away. Tooth decay is caused by **bacteria** in the mouth. Bacteria are tiny one-celled organisms or germs found in the **saliva** or spit in your mouth. Bacteria are too small for you to see.

Bacteria continually multiply and stick to your teeth. This sticky film is called **plaque** (plak). Plaque is colorless and invisible.

When you eat, bits of food stick to this plaque. Bacteria especially thrive on sugary food. When bacteria in the plaque eat the sugar, acid is formed. This acid makes tiny holes in the enamel of your tooth. As more acid is made, the holes get bigger and deeper. Your tooth begins to decay, and you have a **cavity**.

You can help prevent cavities by brushing and flossing your teeth every day. This way, you can remove the plaque before it builds up. Built-up plaque is hard and rough. New plaque hides in the old plaque where it is hard to remove.

# What Causes Gum Disease?

In order to have strong teeth, you need healthy gums. Brushing and flossing your teeth daily helps get rid of the bacteria in plaque that can infect your gums. Here's what happens when your gums get infected:

1. Plaque left on your teeth makes your gums red and sore. They may bleed easily.

2. This soreness can spread deep into your gums.

3. A deep gap or space, sometimes called a "pocket," can form between your tooth and gum.

4. Plaque that is hard to remove builds up in the space between the gum and tooth and continues to infect the gum and finally the jawbone.

5. When the jawbone gets infected, the tooth may become loose and have to be removed.

That's why it is so important to remove plaque before it has a chance to build up on your teeth.

PLAQUE - YUCK!

Meet Your Teeth
© The Learning Works, Inc.

# How to Brush Your Teeth

When you brush your teeth, be gentle and take your time. Use a small, soft toothbrush.

To help reach plaque hiding beneath the gum line, place the toothbrush against your teeth at an **angle** with the bristles pointed toward your gum and make **tiny circles** as shown in the illustration on the right.

Be sure to brush all sides of all your teeth. Think of making three big circles of tiny circles around your mouth: one on the outsides of your teeth, the second on the insides, and the third on the biting surfaces. Here's how:

## CIRCLE #1: OUTSIDES

- With the toothbrush angled toward your gum line, make tiny circles on the outside of your upper tooth. Keep making tiny circles while you move your toothbrush very slowly across the outside of your upper teeth, one tooth at a time.

- Now brush the outside of your lower teeth in the same way.

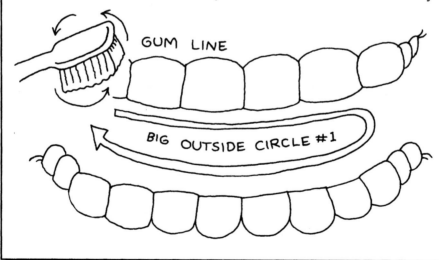

# How to Brush Your Teeth
## (continued)

### CIRCLE #2: INSIDES

- Next, make your tiny circles on the insides of all your teeth all the way around your mouth. Start on a back upper tooth and go to the other side of your mouth.

- Now brush the inside surfaces of your lower teeth. Remember to keep the tips of your brush pointed toward your gum line.

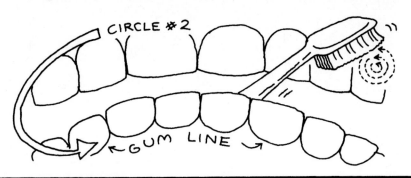

### CIRCLE #3: BITING SURFACES

- Go slowly around your mouth making circles on all biting surfaces.

- When you have finished brushing all of your teeth, brush your tongue. Then rinse your mouth with cool water. Swish and spit until clear water comes out. Rinsing is important because it removes food and plaque that your toothbrush loosened.

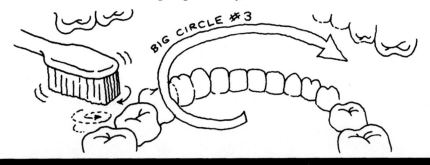

REMEMBER: Circle brushing may feel awkward at first, but with practice you will become comfortable doing it.

Meet Your Teeth
© The Learning Works, Inc.

# Hidden Toothbrushes

Find and color the twelve toothbrushes hidden in the picture.

# Spelling Check-Up

It's time to check up on your spelling. Find and circle the correct spelling of each of the following dental words.

1. a. goms
   b. gums
   c. gumms
   d. gumes

2. a. toth
   b. tuth
   c. tooth
   d. touth

3. a. nerve
   b. nerv
   c. nurve
   d. nirve

4. a. brosh
   b. brush
   c. bruch
   d. broosh

5. a. rote
   b. roote
   c. root
   d. rute

6. a. flos
   b. flose
   c. floos
   d. floss

7. a. enamel
   b. enamal
   c. enamul
   d. enemal

8. a. placue
   b. plak
   c. plaque
   d. plakue

9. a. dentust
   b. dentest
   c. dintist
   d. dentist

10. a. cavety
    b. cavity
    c. caviti
    d. cavaty

# How to Floss

Dental floss is a thin string or tape that can get into places that your toothbrush can't reach. Floss can go under your gum line and in the tight spaces between your teeth.

In order to keep your teeth and gums healthy, it is important to floss your teeth every night before you go to bed.

First, wrap the floss around your fingers like this:

Now you are ready to make a flossing circle around your mouth just as you did for brushing.

**FLOSS LOWER TEETH LIKE THIS:**

1. With the floss around your fingers as above, make a small working area of floss using your thumb and forefinger (first finger) like this:

2. Place the working area between two lower teeth. Gently move the floss back and forth until it slides between the two teeth and just touches your gum. Never use force as you could cut or scrape your gum.

# How to Floss
## (continued)

3. Bring the floss around one of the teeth, making a "C" around the tooth. Now move the floss slowly back and forth, going up and down the tooth.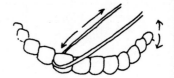

4. Next make a "C" around the tooth on the other side of the floss and move the floss slowly back and forth, going up and down that tooth.

5. Now floss your upper teeth using the same method.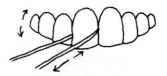

HINT: As you make your flossing circle around your mouth, remember to floss the back side of each back tooth. To do this, hook the floss around the back of the back tooth. Then move the floss back and forth and up and down the same as you do for the other teeth.

ONE FINAL STEP: After flossing, be sure to rinse all the loose plaque away. Swish with fresh, cool water as hard as you can several times.

# My Brush and Floss Chart

Draw a happy face on a tooth each time you brush and floss.

| | Sunday | Monday | Tuesday | Wednesday | Thursday | Friday | Saturday |
|---|---|---|---|---|---|---|---|
| **BRUSH** | | | | | | | |
| **FLOSS** | | | | | | | |

| | Sunday | Monday | Tuesday | Wednesday | Thursday | Friday | Saturday |
|---|---|---|---|---|---|---|---|
| **BRUSH** | | | | | | | |
| **FLOSS** | | | | | | | |

# Foaming at the Mouth

Put some zip and fun into brushing your teeth
by trying this fun experiment.

## WHAT YOU NEED

- toothpaste
- a toothbrush
- tap water
- a bottle of carbonated mineral water or club soda (be sure it's fresh)
- a cup or glass

## WHAT YOU DO

1. Brush the teeth on one side of your mouth with toothpaste.

2. Rinse your mouth with tap water.

3. Now brush the teeth on the other half of your mouth with toothpaste.

4. Rinse your mouth with the carbonated mineral water or club soda instead of tap water.

5. Watch what happens!

### JUST FOR FUN

How can you tell if you are doing a good job of brushing and flossing your teeth?

The answer is disclosing tablets. These tables contain a red dye. When you chew a tablet, the red dye sticks to any unclean areas of your teeth. It discloses, or shows, where the plaque is. You can then brush and floss these areas again.

You can get disclosing tablets from your dentist or local drug store.

# Good Nutrition for Teeth and Gums

Good nutrition for your teeth and gums begins with good nutrition for your whole body. The **Food Guide Pyramid** (PEER-a-mid) is shown on the opposite page.

- The foods at the bottom of the pyramid are made from grains like wheat, oats, corn, and rice. Grains have a lot of **vitamin B** which is important for healthy gums and nerves.

- The next sections contain fruits and vegetables. Color them. Do you eat a lot of fruits and vegetables? If you do, you're probably getting lots of vitamins.

- A very important vitamin in fruits is **vitamin C**. Vitamin C helps your body fight germs, and germs are what cause gum disease. Tomatoes and **citrus fruits**, like oranges and grapefruit, contain a lot of vitamin C.

- An important mineral in green vegetables is **calcium** (KAL-see-um). You also get a lot of calcium from milk, yogurt, and cheese. Calcium helps make strong tooth enamel.

- Foods in the next two sections (such as milk, eggs, fish, and meat) contain **protein** (PRO-teen). Protein is needed to help your body to grow and repair itself and for healthy gums.

- Fats, oils, and sweets are at the top of the pyramid. A healthy diet is one that is low in fat and sugar.

# The Food Guide Pyramid:
# A Guide to Daily Food Choices

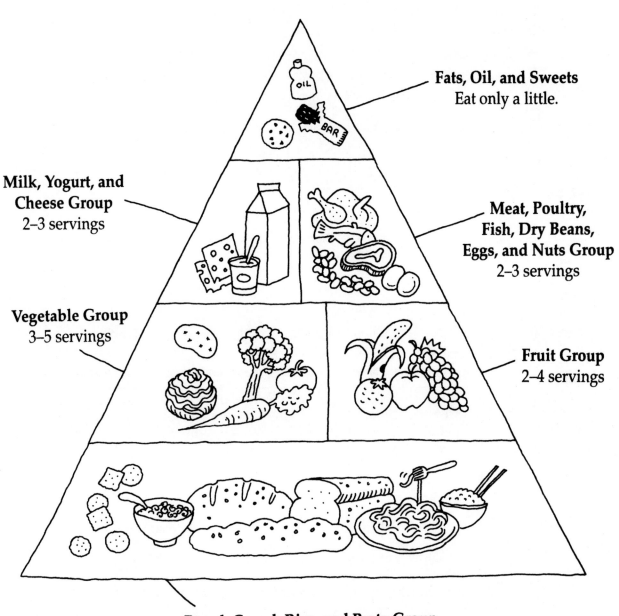

**Fats, Oil, and Sweets**
Eat only a little.

**Milk, Yogurt, and Cheese Group**
2–3 servings

**Meat, Poultry, Fish, Dry Beans, Eggs, and Nuts Group**
2–3 servings

**Vegetable Group**
3–5 servings

**Fruit Group**
2–4 servings

**Bread, Cereal, Rice, and Pasta Group**
6–11 servings

# An Ounce of Prevention

You are very lucky to be a kid of the 90's! We know so much more today about how to keep teeth and gums healthy than when your grandparents were children. That's why some grandparents have lost their teeth and now wear false teeth, called **dentures**.

If you take good care of your teeth, you should have strong, healthy teeth all your life. Here are some DOs and DON'Ts that can help prevent tooth decay and gum disease:

DON'T chew on hard or sharp objects, such as pencils, pens, paper clips, hard candy, and toothpicks. These items could injure your teeth and gums.

DON'T clench or grind your teeth. The pressure can damage and wear down the enamel of your teeth. Ask your parents if you do this in your sleep. If you do, tell your dentist.

DON'T be a mouth breather. Mouth breathing can dry and chap your gums.

DON'T suck on lemons. Lemons have a lot of acid and this acid can dissolve or wash away your tooth enamel.

DO brush, floss, and rinse every night before you go to bed. Try to brush after every meal. If you can't, swish with water until your mouth feels clean.

DO eat a balanced diet, especially foods that you learned about on page 20 that contain protein, calcium, and vitamins B and C.

DO get plenty of sleep. Your body repairs itself while you are asleep.

DO get plenty of exercise, laughter, play, and relaxation. These kinds of activities send "I'm happy" messages to your brain that cause your brain to send "be healthy" messages to all parts of your body.

DO get regular dental check-ups at least every six months.

# Tooth Scramble

Unscramble these words to name the parts of a tooth.
Write the words on the lines below. Use the clue box if you need help.

**CLUE BOX**

| | |
|---|---|
| dentin | nerve |
| enamel | pulp |
| gum | root |

1. lemena  _____

2. tinned  _____

3. lupp  _____

4. mug  _____

5. toro  _____

6. vener  _____

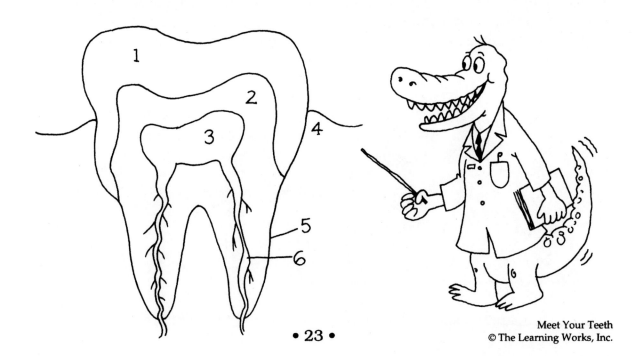

Meet Your Teeth
© The Learning Works, Inc.

# A Dental Exam

You should visit your dentist every six months. During your dental visit, your teeth will be checked to see if you have any cavities, your teeth will be professionally cleaned, and you will probably receive a **fluoride** (FLOOR-ide) treatment (see page 28) to help keep your teeth strong. Here is what a typical visit to the dentist is like:

You will sit in a dental chair that can be adjusted into different positions so the dentist can get a better view of your teeth. A bib will be fastened under your chin to protect your clothes during the exam.

The dentist will check your teeth, gums, tongue, and the inside of your cheeks. An instrument called an **explorer** helps the dentist find holes or cracks in your teeth. The dentist uses a mirror with a long handle to see your back teeth, or molars.

# A Dental Exam
## (continued)

Either the dentist or a dental **hygienist** (hi-JEEN-ist) will clean and polish your teeth. He or she may also give you a fluoride treatment to help prevent cavities.

The dentist may take x-rays to examine teeth that are too close together, to check for cavities that can't be seen, and to check the roots of your teeth. If you have a cavity, the dentist will remove the decay and put in a filling.

By visiting your dentist twice a year for dental check-ups, you can stop small problems from becoming big ones. Regular dental visits help keep your mouth, teeth, and gums healthy.

Meet Your Teeth
© The Learning Works, Inc.

# Find the Way to the Dentist

Help the kids find their way through this maze to the dentist's office.

# An X-Ray of Your Teeth

When the dentist examines your mouth, your teeth may look fine. But your dentist can't see between your teeth or underneath your gums. So the dentist will often have x-rays taken of your teeth to check the roots and to look for hidden cavities.

A lead apron will be placed on your chest to protect you from unnecessary exposure to the x-rays.

A movable arm of the dentist's x-ray machine will then be placed against the outside of your cheek. A piece of film held in place by cardboard will be placed inside your mouth. Sometimes the dentist or the dental assistant will ask you to hold the card in place using one of your fingers. You will be asked to sit without moving for a few seconds while the x-ray is being taken.

The x-ray films will be developed while you wait. On the x-rays, your teeth show up as light grey against a black background. If you have any tooth decay, it will show up as shadows on the light grey portions of the x-ray. Since x-rays can't pass through any **fillings** in your mouth, the fillings will show up as white on the film.

By studying the x-rays, your dentist will be able to spot small or hidden cavities and fill them before they become larger. Next time you visit your dentist, ask him or her to show you one of your x-rays.

# Having Your Teeth Cleaned

Even if you brush and floss your teeth every day, bits of food and plaque can still get caught in the spaces between your teeth and between your gums and teeth. Sometimes this plaque hardens into a substance called **calculus** (KAL-que-lus), or **tartar** (TAR-ter). Tartar is very rough, which makes it easy for more plaque to build up.

You can't remove tartar yourself. When you go to a dentist for a check-up, he or she will clean your teeth and remove any tartar that has built up. Sometimes a dental hygienist will clean and polish your teeth instead of the dentist. The hygienist has been specially trained to clean teeth.

After your teeth have been cleaned and polished, you might be given a fluoride treatment. Fluoride is a chemical that helps make your teeth stronger and harder. To help prevent decay, fluoride is put into the water supply in some cities. You can also buy toothpaste and mouth rinses that contain fluoride.

# How is a Cavity Filled?

A **cavity** is decay in a tooth. If you have a cavity, your dentist will probably take the following steps:

1. The dentist will use a topical anesthetic to numb the area around the cavity. He or she will then give you a shot to make your tooth numb so it has no feeling for a period of time. Even your lip and cheek may become numb. You may feel a little pinch or sting when you get the shot, but you should not feel any discomfort as the dentist works on your tooth.

2. When the medication has taken effect, the dentist will remove the decay.

3. As the dentist works, water is squirted on the tooth.

4. The dentist often places a **suction tube** in your mouth to suck away the water, extra saliva, and decay from your mouth. This helps keep the area dry as the dentist works.

5. After all of the decay is removed, the dentist will replace the decayed part of the tooth with a filling material. The filling can be a silver mixture, plastic, cement, or even gold.

6. Your mouth may feel puffy and numb where the tooth was filled for about an hour or more until the medication wears off.

7. Your dentist will probably tell you not to eat anything for a few hours until the filling hardens or the tooth is no longer numb.

SSSSSSSSSSSSLURRRRP!

• 29 •

# How Are Teeth Straightened?

Straight, evenly-spaced teeth are important not only for a dazzling smile but to help you chew your food properly for digestion. But teeth do not always come in straight. Sometimes teeth . . .

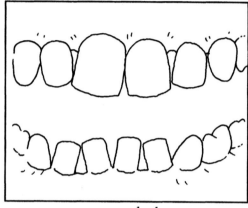
are crooked

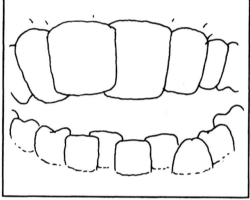
are crowded

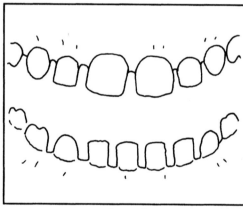
are spaced too far apart

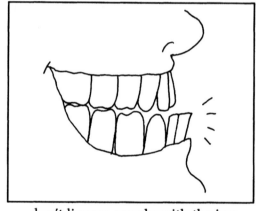
don't line up evenly with the jaw

If you have any of these problems, your dentist will probably suggest that you visit an orthodontist, a dentist who specializes in straightening teeth. After examining your teeth and mouth, an orthodontist will decide on the treatment that is best for you. He or she may fit you with an **appliance**. An appliance is anything you wear in your mouth to help move your jaws and teeth into a better position.

# How Are Teeth Straightened?
## (continued)

Here are some examples of appliances that are worn to help correct crooked or crowded teeth.

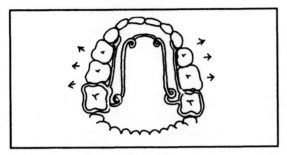

**Palate Spreader.** This appliance helps to widen the roof of the mouth. It helps make room for teeth that are too crowded.

**Headgear.** Headgear helps to move the teeth and jaws into the correct position. There are many different types of headgear. Each style is used for a different bite problem.

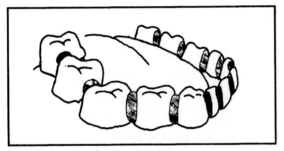

**Spacers.** Spacers are tiny rubber circles that are worn between the teeth to make room for bands. They are usually worn for a week or two before braces are placed on the teeth.

**Bands and Brackets.** Bands are small, thin, metal rings that are cemented to the first molar. Brackets are bonded to all remaining teeth.

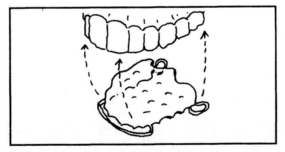

**Retainers.** Retainers hold the teeth in place. They are usually made of plastic and can be removed. A retainer is usually worn after braces have been removed to hold the teeth in their new position. A retainer is also used to help close small spaces between teeth.

Meet Your Teeth
© The Learning Works, Inc.

# First Aid for Teeth

Kids sometimes injure their teeth during sports or while playing.

If you hit a permanent tooth during play, see a dentist as soon as possible. The dentist will look for a chip or crack on the crown of your tooth. He or she will try to wiggle the tooth to be sure that it is not loose and may take an x-ray to be sure there is no damage to the root of your tooth.

If a permanent tooth is accidentally knocked out during play, it is important to find the missing tooth. Many times a dentist can reattach and save the tooth. Here's what you should do:

1. Pick it up carefully by the crown. Do not touch the root.

2. Rinse the tooth gently in cool water. Do not use soap. Do not scrub the tooth with a cloth or brush.

3. Carefully place the rinsed tooth back into its socket and hold it there.

4. If this isn't possible, put the tooth in a glass of cool milk or a cup of water with a teaspoon of salt dissolved in it.

5. Get to a dentist as soon as possible, and remember to take your tooth!

# Fascinating Facts About Teeth

Primary teeth, or baby teeth, start to form about $7\frac{1}{2}$ months *before* a baby is born.

The small bumps you see on some of your teeth are called **cusps**. They help mash your food.

Rats, beavers, and other rodents have teeth that grow all the time.

**Pulp**, which is the name given to the innermost layer of a tooth, is made up of tissue, blood vessels, and nerves.

Tooth enamel is the hardest tissue in your entire body.

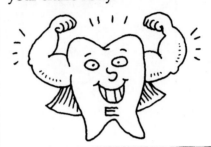

Your upper canines, the sharp pointed teeth next to the incisors, are known as **eyeteeth**.

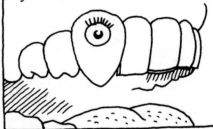

Snakes have teeth that curve back toward their throats. Instead of chewing their prey, they swallow it whole. Snakes use their curved teeth to pull their prey back into their throats.

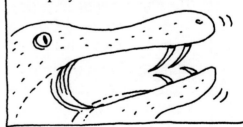

• 33 •

# Snack Smarts

You get home from school and your stomach starts growling. You're hungry, but it's hours until dinner. It's time for a snack!

To keep your teeth healthy, pick a snack that has very little sugar. Here are some yummy snacks that are low in sugar:

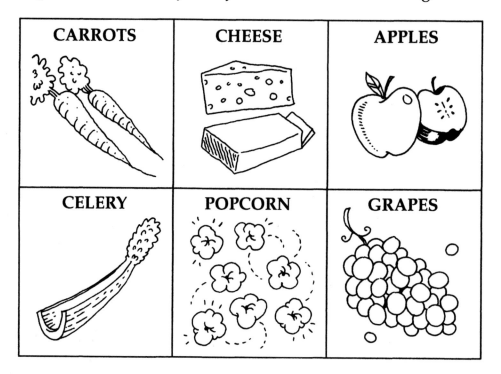

| CARROTS | CHEESE | APPLES |
| CELERY | POPCORN | GRAPES |

### JUST FOR FUN

Be a food detective. Read the labels on packages and cans on your pantry shelves. Make a list of ten foods that contain mostly sugar.

The next time you go grocery shopping with your mom or dad, read the labels and try to select foods that do not have a lot of added sugar.

**Hints for smart detectives:** *Dextrose, maltose, sucrose,* and *glucose* are all names for different kinds of sugar.

# A Healthy Snack

Use the code to color the puzzle below and find a healthy snack to eat.

## CODE BOX

| red | yellow | orange | green | brown |
|-----|--------|--------|-------|-------|
| □ | △ | ○ | ❘ | ✳ |

Meet Your Teeth
© The Learning Works, Inc.

# Crack the Code

Use the following code to solve the mystery sentence below.

**Example:**

T  E  E  T  H

___ ___ ___ ___ ___     ___ ___ ___

___ ___ ___ ___ ___     ___ ___ ___ ___

___ ___ ___ ___ ___ ___     ___ ___ ___ ___ ___ .

# Dental Word Search

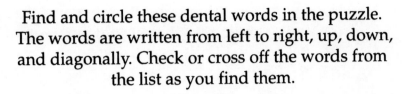

Find and circle these dental words in the puzzle. The words are written from left to right, up, down, and diagonally. Check or cross off the words from the list as you find them.

| ACID | DENTIST | JAW |
| CANINES | ENAMEL | MOLARS |
| CAVITIES | FLOSS | NERVE |
| CROWN | FLUORIDE | PLAQUE |
| DECAY | GUMS | PULP |
| DENTIN | INCISORS | ROOT |

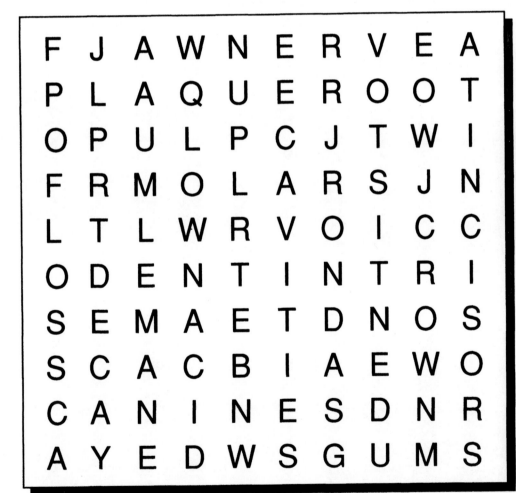

```
F  J  A  W  N  E  R  V  E  A
P  L  A  Q  U  E  R  O  O  T
O  P  U  L  P  C  J  T  W  I
F  R  M  O  L  A  R  S  J  N
L  T  L  W  R  V  O  I  C  C
O  D  E  N  T  I  N  T  R  I
S  E  M  A  E  T  D  N  O  S
S  C  A  C  B  I  A  E  W  O
C  A  N  I  N  E  S  D  N  R
A  Y  E  D  W  S  G  U  M  S
```

Meet Your Teeth
© The Learning Works, Inc.

# Rhyming Word Match-Up

Match up the words in column A with the words that rhyme
in column B. The first one has been done for you.

| A | | B | |
|---|---|---|---|
| 1. | _D_ brush | A. | swerve |
| 2. | _____ drill | B. | smarter |
| 3. | _____ floss | C. | grill |
| 4. | _____ gum | D. | rush |
| 5. | _____ jaw | E. | boot |
| 6. | _____ nerve | F. | booth |
| 7. | _____ pulp | G. | some |
| 8. | _____ root | H. | moss |
| 9. | _____ smile | I. | rack |
| 10. | _____ snack | J. | saw |
| 11. | _____ tartar | K. | gulp |
| 12. | _____ tooth | L. | mile |

# Create a New Toothpaste

Raspberry Sprinkle! Blueberry Bonanza! Peanut Butter and Jelly Swirl! Are these ice cream flavors? No, they're the names of new flavors of toothpaste guaranteed to have kids rushing to brush their teeth three times a day!

Create a new flavor for toothpaste. Give it a "catchy" name, and then design the box for your toothpaste.

LIGHTS! CAMERA! ACTION!

## JUST FOR FUN

- Write a one-minute television commercial for your new toothpaste. Act out your ad for your friends.

- Create a new type of holder for toothbrushes.

- Invent a device that will squeeze the last drop of toothpaste out of the tube.

# How Acid Affects Tooth Enamel

To better understand how acid can dissolve enamel
from your teeth, try this experiment.

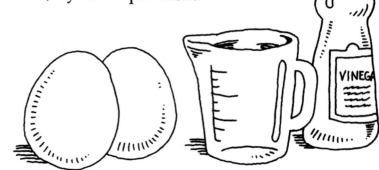

## WHAT YOU NEED

- 2 eggs
- 2 glass measuring cups
- a small covered dish
- white vinegar (an acid)
- water

## WHAT YOU DO

1. Crack a raw egg into the small covered dish. (The shells of eggs are mostly calcium like tooth enamel.) Save the inside to use later in a recipe.

2. Put the eggshell into one of the glass measuring cups.

3. Put enough vinegar into the cup to cover the eggshell.

4. Crack the second egg into the small covered dish and place the dish in the refrigerator.

5. Put the eggshell into the second glass measuring cup.

6. Pour enough water into the cup to cover the eggshell.

7. Wash your hands with soap and water.

8. After several days, check both cups of eggshell. What happened to each eggshell?

9. Leave the eggshell in the vinegar until all the vinegar evaporates or disappears. Watch what happens to the eggshell.

# Sink Your Teeth Into These

**Teachers:** Use this open-ended worksheet to create your own math, spelling, or vocabulary activities. It's great for reinforcing concepts presented in class, for homework assignments, or for extra credit fun for your students.

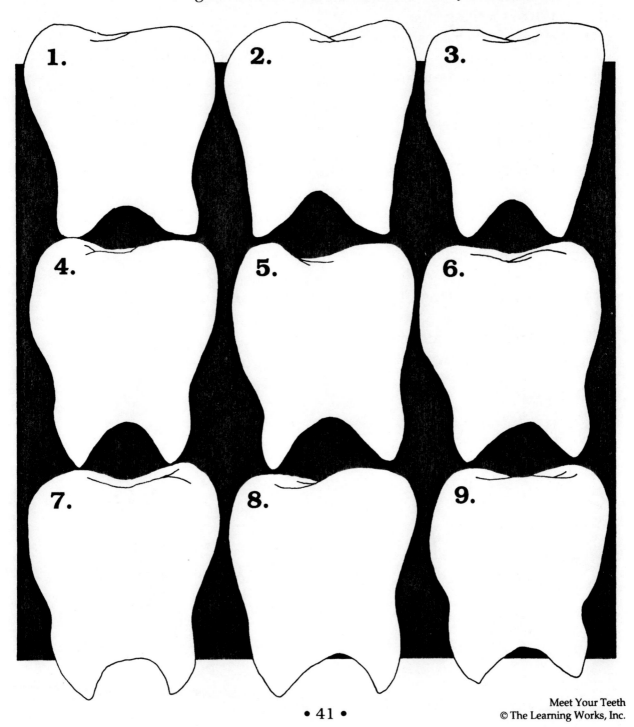

1.

2.

3.

4.

5.

6.

7.

8.

9.

Meet Your Teeth
© The Learning Works, Inc.

# Toothpaste Box Creatures

Make a creature from recycled toothpaste boxes.

## WHAT YOU NEED

- two empty toothpaste boxes that are the same size
- a roll of masking tape
- a sheet of art or construction paper
- a pair of scissors
- crayons or felt-tipped marking pens
- glue

## WHAT YOU DO

1. Cut off one end of each toothpaste box.

2. Stack one box on top of the other with the open ends together.

3. Use tape to hinge the boxes together as shown.

4. Add ears, eyes, fangs, teeth, tongues, and horns.

5. Draw, color, cut out, and attach a paper body to your creature's head. Use the pattern on page 43.

# Toothpaste Box Creatures
## (continued)

Use this pattern for the body of your Toothpaste Box Creature.
Tape the head of your creature to the body.

Meet Your Teeth
© The Learning Works, Inc.

# Pint-Size Puppets

Make a copy of this page. Then color the finger puppets, cut them out, tape the ends together, and have fun! Get together with your friends and create original skits. Perform your skits for other kids so they learn more about dental health.

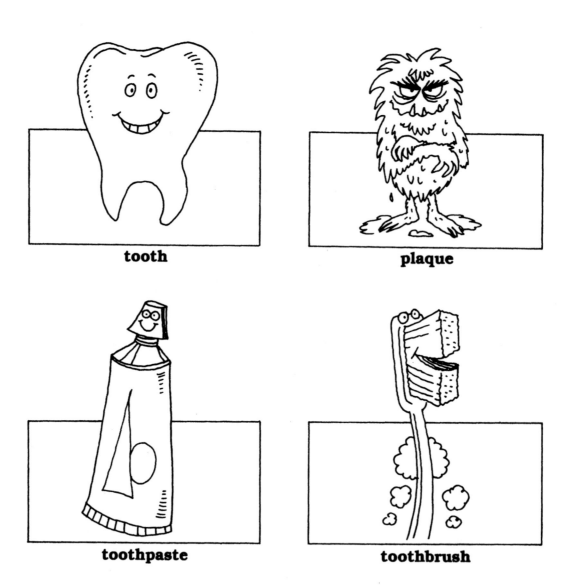

**tooth**

**plaque**

**toothpaste**

**toothbrush**

# Create a Poster

Create a poster in honor of National Dental Hygiene Week in October or National Children's Dental Health Month in February by following these steps.

1. Pick a simple theme for your poster. It should be a message you think is important. Here are some suggestions:

   - Brush Them or Lose Them
   - Floss Every Day
   - Eat Healthy for Healthy Teeth
   - Visit Your Dentist Twice a Year
   - Fight Cavities by Brushing
   - Protect Your Teeth During Sports

2. Write your theme on your poster in large letters.

3. Draw and color pictures to illustrate the theme of your poster.

4. You can also use magazine pictures. Find, cut out, and paste the pictures on your poster.

5. Display your poster in your classroom for others to see.

• 45 •

# Careers in Dentistry

There are many choices open to women and men interested in dentistry as a career. Here are a few you might consider when you get older.

### GENERAL DENTIST

**General dentists** (usually called just "dentists") help us keep our teeth and gums healthy and teach us how to prevent diseases of the mouth. They give dental check-ups, fill cavities, take dental x-rays, replace lost teeth with **dentures** and sometimes pull teeth.

### ORTHODONTIST

**Orthodontists** are dentists whose practice is limited to the correction of the teeth and jaws.

### DENTAL HYGIENIST

**Dental hygienists** are trained to clean and polish our teeth with special instruments. They also teach us the proper way to brush and floss to keep our teeth and gums healthy.

# Careers in Dentistry
## (continued)

Here are some other dental career choices you might want to consider when you are older.

### PEDODONTIST

**Pedodontists** (PEE-do-don-tists) are dentists who specialize in working with children. They give dental check-ups, fill cavities, and make sure that children's gums are healthy. They sometimes clean teeth.

### PERIODONTIST

**Periodontists** are dentists who specialize in preventing and treating gum disease. They also deal with diseases of the bones around the teeth.

### SERVICE TECHNICIAN

**Dental service technicians** install new equipment in dental offices and repair it to keep it working properly.

These are just a few of the career choices open to you in the field of dentistry. Here is a list of other people that either help in a dentist's office or have jobs related to the dental field:

- office receptionist
- office bookkeeper
- dental assistant
- oral surgeon
- dental laboratory technician
- dental instructor or professor

Your library will have books you can read to find out more about these and other careers in dentistry.

Meet Your Teeth
© The Learning Works, Inc.

# Bookmarks

**Teachers:**  Copy and cut out these bookmarks for your students to color. These bookmarks are fun to use all year long or to give as gifts during National Dental Hygiene Week or National Children's Dental Health Month.

# Bulletin Board Idea

**Teachers:** Using the shapes shown below as patterns, draw and cut out a toothbrush and a tube of toothpaste. Post them on the board with a diagram of the cross-section of a tooth. Add numbers as shown. Write the name of each part of the tooth on an index card. Put the cards in an envelope. Label the envelope "cards" and post it on the board. For self-checking, make available a key on which tooth parts are listed and identified by number or write the corresponding number on the back of each word card.

Encourage students to label the tooth parts by taking the cards from the envelope and attaching them to the board on or near the appropriate numbers.

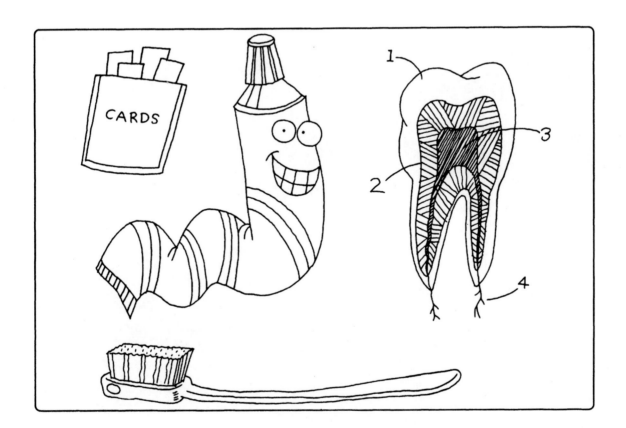

Meet Your Teeth
© The Learning Works, Inc.

# Dental Clip Art

**Teachers:**  Here is some clip art for you to copy and cut out. Use the pictures on letters home during National Children's Dental Health Month in February. You and your students can also use them to decorate memos, worksheets, or bulletin boards.

# Awards

**Teachers:** Copy these awards on colored construction paper, cut them out, and present them to your students.

_____

has earned the

## SUPER DUPER BRUSHER AWARD

## Super Smile Award presented to

_____

## The Fantastic Flosser Award

**is presented to**

_____

The Sparkling Teeth Award goes to

_____

Meet Your Teeth
© The Learning Works, Inc.

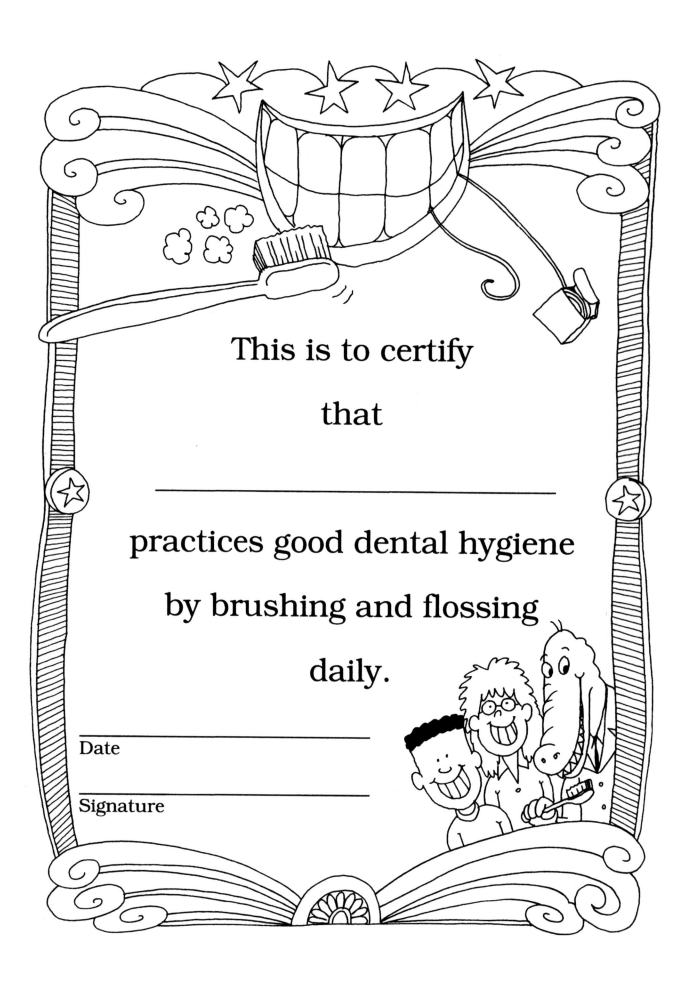

This is to certify

that

_____

practices good dental hygiene

by brushing and flossing

daily.

_____
Date

_____
Signature

# A Dental Dictionary

**acid**  Acid is made when the bacteria in plaque feed on sugar in food. This acid makes holes in the enamel of the tooth.

**baby teeth**  Baby teeth are also known as primary teeth or milk teeth. These twenty teeth make up the first set of teeth and usually start erupting or breaking through the gums at five or six months of age.

**bacteria**  Bacteria are invisible, one-celled organisms found in the mouth and in other parts of the body.

**bicuspids**  Bicuspids are teeth that have two sharp points that help crunch and shred food. They are located between the canines and the molars.

**blood vessels**  Blood vessels are tubes that carry blood over the body. They are found inside each tooth.

**braces**  Braces are metal strips attached to the teeth and connected by rubber bands and springy wires that are gradually tightened to straighten crooked teeth.

**calculus**  Calculus or tartar, is plaque that has hardened on the teeth and gums.

**cavity**  A cavity is a hole in a tooth caused by decay.

**crown**  The crown is the shiny, upper part of the tooth above the gum. It is the only part of the tooth that you can see.

**cuspids**  Cuspids, or canines, are the pointed teeth next to the incisors that are used to tear food.

**cusps**  Cusps are the small bumps on the biting surface of teeth that help mash food.

**decay**  Decay is the rotting away of a tooth. It starts on the enamel of the tooth and can spread to the dentin and pulp.

**dental floss**  Dental floss is a fine thread or tape used for cleaning between teeth and under the gums.

BRACES

FLOSS

• 53 •

# A Dental Dictionary
## (continued)

**dental x-ray**  A dental x-ray is a special kind of picture that shows your teeth and jawbone but not your cheeks, lips, tongue, or other soft tissues.

**dentin**  Dentin is the hard layer of the tooth under the enamel.

**dentist**  A dentist is a doctor who specializes in treating the teeth, gums, and mouth.

**dentures**  Dentures are false teeth worn by people who have had their teeth removed because of injury, tooth decay, or gum disease.

**disclosing tablets**  Disclosing tablets are tablets made with a food dye that stains plaque on teeth so it can be seen and removed.

**enamel**  Enamel is the shiny white layer on the outside of a tooth that covers the crown. It is the hardest substance in the body.

**erupt**  Erupt is the term given to teeth growing through the gums. The first tooth usually erupts at about five or six months of age.

**explorer**  An explorer is a special instrument used by dentists and dental hygienists to check your teeth and gums for cavities and pockets.

**fluoride**  Fluoride is a chemical that helps make teeth strong and prevents decay. It can be found in water and in most toothpastes.

**gum disease**  Gum disease is caused by bacteria in plaque that infect gum tissue, making holes, or pockets, between the tooth root and the gum. If gum disease is not treated, it can infect the jawbone.

**gums**  Gums are the thin layers of flesh that cover the jawbone and the roots of teeth. Gums are also called gingiva.

**incisors**  Incisors are the sharp, pointed front teeth that are used for cutting food.

**hygienist**  A hygienist is a person specially trained to clean teeth.

INCISORS

X-RAY

WISDOM TOOTH

# A Dental Dictionary
## (continued)

| | |
|---|---|
| **molars** | Molars are the back teeth that are used for grinding food. |
| **nerves** | Nerves carry messages to and from the brain. |
| **orthodontist** | An orthodontist is a dentist who straightens teeth and corrects how teeth fit together when you bite and chew. |
| **pedodontist** | A pedodontist is a dentist who treats children. |
| **periodontist** | A periodontist is a dentist who prevents and treats gum and jawbone disease. |
| **permanent teeth** | Permanent teeth replace the primary, or baby teeth. There are usually 32 permanent teeth. |
| **plaque** | Plaque is a thin layer of colorless, invisible bacteria found on the teeth. |
| **pocket** | A pocket is a deep space between the gum and root of a tooth. It is caused by gum disease. |
| **pulp** | Pulp is the soft middle part of a tooth that contains nerves and blood vessels. |
| **root** | The root of a tooth is fixed to the jawbone and is under the gum. |
| **saliva** | Saliva is the liquid found in the mouth that wets food as it is chewed, making it easier to swallow. |
| **service technician** | A dental service technician is trained to install and repair the types of equipment found in a dentist's office. |
| **socket** | A socket is the place in the jawbone that holds a tooth. |
| **wisdom teeth** | Wisdom teeth are the last molars to erupt, usually at age 17 or 18. In some people, the wisdom teeth never erupt. |

Meet Your Teeth
© The Learning Works, Inc.

# Answer Key

## Page 14 • Hidden Toothbrushes

## Page 15 • Spelling Check-Up

| | | |
|---|---|---|
| 1. b | 5. c | 9. d |
| 2. c | 6. d | 10. b |
| 3. a | 7. a | |
| 4. b | 8. c | |

## Page 23 • Tooth Scramble

| | |
|---|---|
| 1. enamel | 4. gum |
| 2. dentin | 5. root |
| 3. pulp | 6. nerve |

## Page 26 • Find the Way to the Dentist

## Page 35 • A Healthy Snack

The hidden picture is of a plate of apples.

## Page 36 • Crack the Code

Brush and floss your teeth daily.

## Page 37 • Dental Word Search

| F | J | A | W | N | E | R | V | E | A | A |
|---|---|---|---|---|---|---|---|---|---|---|
| P | L | A | Q | U | E | R | O | O | T | |
| O | P | U | L | P | C | J | T | W | I | |
| F | R | M | O | L | A | R | S | J | N | |
| L | T | L | W | R | V | O | I | C | C | |
| O | D | E | N | T | I | N | T | R | I | |
| S | E | M | A | E | T | D | N | O | S | |
| S | C | A | C | B | I | A | E | W | O | |
| C | A | N | I | N | E | S | D | N | R | |
| A | Y | E | D | W | S | G | U | M | S | |

## Page 38 • Rhyming Word Match-Up

| | | | |
|---|---|---|---|
| 1. D | | 7. K | |
| 2. C | | 8. E | |
| 3. H | | 9. L | |
| 4. G | | 10. I | |
| 5. J | | 11. B | |
| 6. A | | 12. F | |